## Introduction

My life of debt began just like everyone else's. At the tender age of 18, I got my first credit card. Then my second. Then my third. It was time to go to college and my car broke down. Instead of paying the $3,000.00 repair quote that I could not afford, I decided it would be a better idea to buy a new car for $16,000.00 because I could afford the "payments". My mother made $6.00 too much the previous tax year in order for me to qualify for a grant for school. So, an additional $22,000.00 student loan went on the bill.

I graduated with a 4.0 GPA and honors from my class with an associate's degree in computer technology and a minor in electronics. I graduated 1 month after the dot com bubble burst and the economy went into a deep recession. Later, the college I went to went bankrupt and out of business. So my degree counted for nothing. $22,000.00 spent and nothing to show for it.

I got whatever job I could, as close to my field as I could find. Closest I could find was $12.00 an hour as a customer service agent at a mom-and-pop shop that did electronics calibrations for large corporations. I didn't see a raise for years. Time went on and I just kept using my credit cards, paying the minimum along with my car payment. Fannie Mae was kind enough to send me a notice stating I was able to defer my payments if I wanted. So I did it.

What I didn't realize at my young age was that the $3,000.00 car repair could have been done for $600.00 at a shop that did not charge such outrageous markups on parts and labor. Shops take advantage of young women, and this particular shop was taking advantage. What I also didn't realize is the amazingly kind and wonderful Fannie Mae was still accumulating interest on my student loan which was not in the paperwork they sent me.

After getting home from work one day, ALL of my bills came in at once, with fine print and all. For the first time at the age of 20, I decided to read it instead of just pay the minimum and go about my business. I guess I was bored that night. When I added everything up, I still owed $14,000.00 on my car, $14,000.00 on my credit cards and $21,000.00 on my student loan. WHAT?!?! I owe $49,000.00?!?!? Oh, hell no! It was my a-ha moment. My mother always tried to teach me about debt, amortization schedules on a mortgage, how credit cards are bad and debt is bad. I never listened but always had a high level of integrity. My word was my bond. I promised to pay these companies back. And I absolutely hated owing that much. Even during the great recession, I went out the very next day and got a 2nd job. Please keep in mind that at the age of 18, I did what my momma told me and put $250 into my 401k and forgot about it...just like she told me to.

After taking on the second job, I was now working 6:00 am until midnight 6 days a week. On the 7th day, I still had a 6 hour shift. If not, I would go to the Labor Ready places and work a shift for chump change. I didn't care. I was driven. I was focused. I was NOT going to owe these people and I was NEVER going to allow this happen again.

For a year and a half, I worked and slaved and didn't buy anything. No clothes, no internet, no cable TV, no cell phone. Just rent, food, gas and utilities. Even then, I was heavily relying on company potlucks to feed me. It was not on purpose at all, but I was so stressed, broke and busy that I had forgotten to eat. Every single penny went towards my debt. I started with getting rid of my credit cards, then my car, then my student loans. I didn't know this at the time, but I was getting rid of the right debt in the proper order.

In the middle of all this working, I got a phone call from the leasing office of my apartment complex. My roommate and I paid our rent separately and he was not paying his half. They stated they had put notices on the door for months. I told them I worked from 6:00 am until midnight every day and didn't see any notices. My roommate, knowing he was not paying rent, was taking down the notices and not telling me. So...I had to break the lease. I could not afford the apartment on my own. There goes $2,500.00 that I didn't have and I had no place to go. I asked my mother if I could stay with her for a couple weeks until I could find a new apartment without a roommate. She said no. She said you are coming to stay with me until you are completely debt free. It took me 6 months of living with her and only a week to find an apartment I could afford once the debt was all paid off. I did pay a very small amount of rent as well as utilities during this time to help cover the bills. I insisted on doing so while my mother insisted I don't. I paid maybe $150 a month, which was nothing. It was pretty much the extra $50 I was using in electricity plus an extra $100 just for taking up space. Again, my mother didn't want me to pay anything but Insisted. While I was there I was also able to help her with things around the house like mowing the lawn, cooking, cleaning the house, painting, cleaning out gutters and organizing and things like that. I even installed a new water heater for the first time while I was there. All by myself and I was darn proud of it!

While getting out of debt, everyone at both of my jobs knew what I was doing and rooted me on! "You can do it girl!" It was motivating and made me feel like I was doing the right thing. I made $1,000.00 payments at a time and finally...I was debt free. I even overpaid them a little and got a $16.00 check from them months later. I remember taking my statement to my co-worker Kim and she gave me a huge high-five and a hug when I became debt free. It was a great feeling and I would do everything I could to never get back into debt again.

I moved into an adorable apartment all by myself. Meaning, I didn't have to rely on a roommate to pay their half of the rent and leaving me in the dark. I was now 22. The apartment complex was an 8-plex and built in the 1940's. It was privately owned and the kitchen seemed like it had never been updated, other than the refrigerator and oven. I LOVED IT! I had huge windows outside the kitchen looking into two pine trees that had naturally created a tunnel that led to a small back area where apartment dwellers were encouraged to hang their laundry. The apartment complex had a laundry line set up with clothes pins and all. There was also a small area behind the clothesline that was growing organic grapes along the fence line. I could do my wash, hang dry my clothes and sit out there and read a book and eat grapes right off the vine in complete bliss. I loved that place. I always tell myself If I ever win the lottery, I am buying that complex and moving back into my old apartment. I was only a mile away from my Mom In one direction, and a mile away from my brother in the other. I never went into debt again.

Let's fast forward a bit. My mother passed away when I was 28. While living on my own in the apartment, I had become accustomed to not spending any money and working 2 jobs. So, I just kept going. I continued for years working 2 jobs from 6:00 am until midnight and the money just piled up, along with my 401k contributions being quadrupled. Even living on my own, paying rent, having internet and everything I wanted, the money accumulated and accumulated. I started looking for a house of my own because by this time I had enough for a very hefty down payment in the area. Then my mother died.

When my mother died, my brother and I were to inherit the house. I was taking care of her already while living in my apartment so my brother told me I could have it. I moved in. I can not begin to tell you how emotionally devastated I was. She died on 2/12/2010. With an inheritance, you don't just get to keep everything without issue. With a living will and trust, which is what she had, you get everything she had, but you also owe everything she owed. She still owed $40,000.00 on the house. With the money I was saving with for a down payment for my own house, I paid it off. Then the recession came. Within one month I had lost my mother and my jobs. Both of them. I was in the house I grew up in and that helped. It felt like home.

My mother had some hoarding issues and that was very expensive to remove. There were a lot of issues with the house that had been neglected like the roof, flooring and walls. To honor my mother's memory, I wanted her house to be as beautiful as possible. So I repaired all of those issues in cash and kept as many useful items of hers as I could to decorate the house. All in all, I spent about $40k on paying off the house, $100k in repairs and $40k in property taxes over the years. So I put in $180k into my mom's house.

Another recession in full bloom and my mother just dying, I took unemployment for as long as I could. Even though the unemployment checks were only $1800 per month, I was still putting $1,000 per month towards my retirement. My Mom really engrained that into me. She told me not to stop, don't look at it, just do it. Anyway, my unemployment had been extended to a year and a half and I believe I was around a year and a month when I found a job at a large furniture company in a call center for $10.00 an hour. Yup. Years had passed and I was now making less than I was in my early 20's. Well...back to extreme money saving it was. I read every single book I could at the library about scrimping and saving and not spending and debt freedom. I perfected the art. That is correct. Money saving is an art form that few are able to master. Well, I did. Some think I am a miser. Some think that I live a horrible life. But most just do not understand the unknown. Debt freedom these days is the unknown. Not spending but still being happy is very unknown to people. We are no longer citizens of the United States of America. We are known as consumers. Is that what you want to be known as? A consumer? These were the penny pinching times that taught me everything I know.

While living in my mother's house after she passed away I just kept working and accumulating more. After 9 years of living there with insanely high property taxes and bills in the Bay Area of California, making a low wave, I was still able to save $100,000.00 (not including my retirement savings). My brother had his own life. A huge 2,900 sq. ft. house in the Bay Area, 4 kids and a job making six figures. He decided he wanted to sell the house and get his share. He would not allow me to buy him out. Please note, I offered far more than the $100,000.00 I had saved and was even willing to get back into debt to keep the family home. So I was given 6 months to fix up the place even more to get the most money when the time came to sell. Turns out it would sell in 2 months. There was no way I could afford a house in the Bay Area of California on my salary. Right when my brother told me we were selling the house I got bag-lady syndrome and bought a cheap house in Arizona for $67,000.00 with low property taxes of $450.00 per year. I was terrified of being homeless. Mostly because I had a dog, and was scared I would have to give him away. Now I am living in a 900 sq. ft. home with my dog and a fully fenced back yard while working online. When it comes to the house, I put in $180k and my share of the sale was $292k. That money was invested into retirement as well. I didn't need it. That is another story to be told.

Let's get to the extreme cost saving measures I learned and how you can do it too and still maintain your lifestyle without any suffering.

CHAPTER 1

# AFTER THE STORM

Once you get all the debt paid off, life gets so much easier. Let me guess. You think that living a debt-free life full of drudgery, working 12 hours a day, living in a cave somewhere in the mountains. Or maybe you think it is a life without socializing, eating out or you will have a never-ending claustrophobic feeling where you are unable to spend on anything you want. Maybe you think that you will have to decorate your house with cast-offs or garbage that somebody else didn't want, where your roof is falling apart and your lawn is dead because you couldn't afford the water bill. Or maybe you think that you will look like an 80's wannabe with horrible clothes that are in rags that you got in the church basement because it is all you could afford. If you are female, maybe you think you won't be able to wear makeup or have any jewelry or accessories. In doing so, society will cast you out as someone that is somehow unintelligent because of course, you lack the intelligence to look half way put together. If you are male, maybe you think that women won't want to date you because your car is old and dented and smoking because when you are frugal, of course you never spend money on your car, let alone spend money on a date. I get it. You are scared. It is okay. I was there at one time too. People have a tendency to fear the unknown, and you have never been debt-free. So you don't know what it is like. Well let me tell you that it is exactly the opposite of what you are thinking.

Let me walk you through my home. It is a simple 900 sq. ft. 2 bedroom/2 bathroom home in the desert only blocks from the Colorado River, shopping and the library. Walking to any location is just a matter of putting on a backpack. This place needs work, but I just got here. When walking in the door you immediately enter the living room and dining area. An open concept with neutral walls and decorated in mid-century modern furnishings along with modern abstract artwork, most of which were either gotten at a thrift store or on clearance at a place like TJ Maxx or Ross. The windows are luxuriously decorated in light grey black-out curtains to help save on electricity costs. Pops of color direct your eye to a 1950's Cigar Leather sitting chair given by my Grandmother. A nearly aqua blue console holds the library with only a small lamp on top gotten out of the garbage and an LCD bulb using only 9 watts to save on electricity.

There is a small working fireplace filled with a stack of wood sitting inside just waiting for winter. The ambiance of a fire burning is greatly appreciated during those cold winter nights. Yes, it gets cold in the desert in the winter.

I love television. I know, I know but I really really do. I have a Vizio 48" Smart TV in the living room located in the corner purchased 7 years ago for around $400.00. Now the same one probably goes for $150.00. One of my luxuries that I do not regret, and I never will.

The small eating area (remember, it's just me) is covered by a black tablecloth given by a friend with luxurious beige modern chairs on each side. These were purchased on amazon for $125.00 for a set of 4. Only 2 are needed, so the other two are in the guest room but we will get to that later. On top of the black tablecloth is a giant bowl brimming with fresh fruit including pineapple, cuties and honeycrisp apples.

The cottage style kitchen is gorgeously decorated with white cabinets and a small apartment sized 11 Cu. Ft. Whirlpool refrigerator. The last one I had was 14 cu. Ft. and always seemed way too big. The 11 Cu. Ft. also saves a great deal of electricity and can easily be powered via the solar system in the backyard. A bowl of sweet potatoes sits on the countertop for the occasional quick dinner. If you open the cabinets you will see stores of organic bread flour, rice, beans, quinoa. Another cabinet holds breakfast foods for the next 6 months that includes only oats, banana chips and organic granola purchased in bulk which only needs to be purchased once a year for about $100.00.

Leading from the kitchen to the hallway is a pantry packed full of emergency food storage and supplies (a serious hobby of mine). To the left in the hallway is the giant guest bedroom which is a converted one car garage with some serious closet space. This room is designed with a luxurious king size bed with Egyptian cotton sheets purchased at a thrift store in the original package for $4.00. The RH grey duvet color to match the headboard was won in a raffle. There is a 42" flat panel LCD Smart TV that was given by a friend that said it was too small. Side tables were purchased at TJ Maxx for $59.00 each and the matching silver table lamps were also from a thrift store. The price of the lamps has long left my mind but these are also supplied with 9 watt LCD bulbs to save on electricity.

Under the window in the guest room is an old plastic outdoor table that was originally intended for small cups of coffee while sitting outside. This was spray painted glossy black for ambiance and the remaining 2 of the set of 4 beige chairs sits at the table to match.

The guest bathroom has artwork hanging above the 3' garden tub that were given by a coworker when I left my last position and moved out of state. There are a couple grey photos of flowers or something above the toilet that were given to me for free by my realtor. Plants that enjoy the bathroom air line the 3' garden tub on each side.

The master bedroom has luxurious black out curtains above the headboard of a queen sized bed frame that has an 1800's look to it. The bed was picked out of the garbage and spray painted black to cover the rust. It now looks brand new. The mattress is another story. One of the few items I always buy brand new. Next to the bed is an antique dresser passed down from the women in my family for 4 generations. The closet and dresser are packed full of designer clothes purchased at thrift stores for pennies on the dollar. My entire wardrobe probably cost $100.00 or less in total yet it is abundantly stocked. Heck, I could probably go for a month without wearing the same thing twice.

The backyard is a work in progress but so far I have planted (yes, in the desert), a fig tree, 8 dragon fruits of two different varieties along with some grapes, watermelon and red bell peppers. All are doing well and in the fall at least 4 fruit trees will be added along with a lawn. Yes, fruit trees and lawns grow in the desert! So in summary, the house is beautifully decorated and the pantry is full. It needs a bit of work but hey, it is paid for. No debt and only $450.00 per year in property taxes. I'll take it!

CHAPTER 2

# HOUSING

Everyone needs a place to live. But does everyone need the 2,000+ sq. ft. 3 bed/2 bath with a large yard that our "culture" has deemed to be the perfect house?

So you believe that your house is your greatest asset? I can tell you right now, it's not. A bit of counter-culture math for you.

You buy a $200,000.00 house.

With a 20% down payment you have a mortgage of $180,000.00.

After 30 years you have paid over $100,000.00 in INTEREST (not the principal of the house).

Your kids leave the nest and you realize the house is too big for you so you sell it. It has "appreciated" because it is an asset. So, you sell it for $300,000.00 and pay the sellers fee of 5%, which is $15,000.00 making a "profit" of $285,000.00. Except with the mortgage interest and down payment, you paid $300,000.00 for it. You lost $15,000.00 even though it "appreciated" in value. See?

After living in the house for over 30 years, your greatest asset didn't make you anything at all. In fact, it lost you money since you took out a mortgage. Don't even get me started on capital gains taxes. See how math works?

Unless you paid for your house in cash right after moving out of your parent's house, you lost money. Why? Because a house is not an investment or an asset. A house is a liability. An asset MAKES you money, a liability COSTS you money. These numbers definitely change if you make more than a 20% down payment and aggressively pay off the mortgage. But if you are just like everyone else, you lost money.

Think outside the box. Be unconventional. Be counter-culture. Let your friend's make fun of you. DO IT! Unless you have an insanely high paying job along with a significant other that ALSO has a high paying job, you need to think small. Maybe a 2 bed/2 bath home with a small yard will work for you and your children, given they are the same sex. There are also many 2 bed/1 bath homes out there. These are far less expensive than the standard 3 bed/2 bath or even 2 bed/2 bath. Why? Because for some reason an "extra" bathroom is sought after. Personally, I have 2 bathrooms and only use 1. The other is for "guests" but I would be more than happy sharing just 1.

I have seen what happens when people get sick. I have seen what happens when people grow old. Large (standard in the American culture) are far too large for a single person to typically handle after the age of 50. I am serious. If you live alone and have a 3 bed/2 bath house with a front and back yard, it wears on you very quickly. Think about it. You have a large kitchen, floors, dusting, window washing, repairs, upkeep, lawn maintenance, gutter cleaning, sweeping, mopping, weeding, updating. It is hard work owning a home. Do I advocate living in an apartment. No way! Not unless you own a duplex or larger and live in one of the apartments for free. I am just saying that there is a possibility that you will grow to an age where it gets to be too much. Have you ever visiting a grandmother or grandfather unexpectedly and found a layer of dust on the record player and television along with tissues sitting all over the coffee table? Dirty dishes in the sink, dirty windows and a refrigerator that is growing a forest? Me too. It is sad. Keep things small and you might not ever have to worry about your house becoming too much for you to care for.

I am here to tell you that large families can live in small houses. If you don't believe me, look on youtube. Thousands of videos titled along the lines of "Family of 7 Live in 500 sq. ft.". Maybe that is too small for you. It would be too small for me too. What is your claustrophobic limit? Mine is 800 sq. ft. for 4 people (2 parents and 2 children. Parents in one room and children in the other). Please note that the average sq. footage of homes built today is around 2,687. In 1973 it was only 1,660 sq. ft. In 1900 it was 700-900 sq. ft. These small homes in 1900 held huge families in a growing nation. Can't we go back there again and save a huge amount of money in the meantime? Yes we can!

If you are still trying to get out of debt, see if you can move in with family and pay rent for a room. If not, rent out a room in your place. If you don't like having a full-time roommate, maybe you can AirBnb an extra room. If you have more than one child and they are the same sex, put a bunk bed in one room and make them share so the 2nd bedroom can be rented. Children are very smart. Tell them exactly what is going on and they will be hesitant, but eventually will be on board.

When buying a home, never look for move-in ready houses. You don't want those. Those are the ones that have been "fixed up" for sale at the highest dollar with new paint and flooring added. The add might say new flooring but they have likely chosen the cheapest snap and bundle flooring you can get for 98 cents a square foot and just put it over the old laminate flooring or cement without pulling the old flooring up.

Freshly painted. Yeah, that's about $200.00 but they raise the price by $5,000.00 for the $200.00 worth of paint. Why? Because it looks pretty.

Updated kitchen? Ha! What does that mean? It means they painted over the old cabinets without sanding them and slapped on some new hardware. Maybe they went all out and spent $250.00 on a new countertop to make it look brand new. Maybe they put some peel and stick tile down over the old laminate. Total cost? About $400.00. But they probably added an extra $8,000.00 to the sticker price of the turn-key move-in ready home.

Updated bathroom? Same thing. Peel and stick tile is my personal favorite and you can literally peel and stick tile on to a concrete bathroom floor for a total of $35.00 to make it look brand new. New vanity? About $150.00 for a really pretty one. Paint? $35.00. I swear, bathroom remodels elude me because they are SO SO easy and cheap to completely remodel. You can get a brand new bath tub shower combo at Home Depot or Lowe's (a really really nice one) for $500.00. Plumbing, maybe another $100.00. If you want the super fancy tile it will cost you extra but that option is your choice, not mine. I prefer simple showers since I'm only stepping in there to get clean anyway. You are looking at a total bathroom remodel for about $800.00, yet they add $10,000.00 to the sticker price of the turn key move in ready home.

Look for the messed up, ugly houses. You make the most money at the time you buy your house, not the time you sell it. Just make sure the foundation, electrical and plumbing are solid. The rest is just smoke and mirrors. Or in this case, paint and flooring. Aside from hiring out for electrical and plumbing (or foundation issues), everything can be done by yourself. Paint and pillows can make a $50,000.00 house look like a $150,000.00 house overnight. Add an herb garden under windowsills or mulch to make it look super fancy. If you want a lawn, I don't blame you. It is the "norm" but these days I much prefer calling a local landscaper for free truck loads of wood chips and planting trees that will provide me with food for free. It's like growing your own money. In the times ahead, many neighborhoods will move away from lawns and into growing food. More and more people every day are realizing that these baby-sized fields of grass that used to indicate abundance and wealth in the 1700's now only lead to their car in the driveway. In the 1700's, lords of the manor would be considered wealthy if they had so much land that they could leave some of it with some useless grass instead of having the farm hands and such use the space for chickens, goats, geese, food and so on. These useless baby-sized fields in modern America take time to mow, time to weed, money to fertilize and gives the owner nothing in return. Time for a change.

If you have poor soil like sand or clay, start calling your local landscapers and arborists to see if they will do a wood chip drop at your house. This will save them the cost of having to take the chips to the local dump, will keep it out of the landfill and if you are able to add 6" of these wood chips to your existing poor soil conditions, it will change the soil completely. The microbes and natural degradation of the wood chips will turn into mulch. Continue watering these wood chips just like you would a regular lawn. After a year it will be ready for planting just about anything. I have seen people growing food forests in the Arizona high desert in Phoenix. Dark rich soil truly is the heartbeat of the planet.

5 gallons of paint and panting supplies (brushes, rollers etc.) for $250.00 or less and you can paint your whole house. My ugly brown house was painted vibrant green with white trim for $250.00 in paint AND paint supplies (paint brushes, tarps, rollers, etc.) Labor is free. Make use of it and increase the value of your ugly house overnight.

A major part of any home is the garden. Even if you have an ugly house, the backyard or garden can make a huge difference in the resale value of the house, personal well-being and your pocket book. Look up your zones and see what you can grow but fruit trees and perennial vegetables provide the most bang for your buck.

In my old California home, the backyard consisted of 3 apple trees, 1 nectarine tree, 2 aloe vera bushes, 4 artichoke bushes, a cherry tree and all of the fences were lined with edible seedless grapes. These were all planted once and provided free food for years. I barely ever pruned them, barely ever did anything with them. All I had to do was plant and water once a week in the summer. In fact, the artichoke plants all came from one single bush. If you leave them alone over winter, they are like weeds and multiply. I simply dug up the new ones and moved them to another part of the yard. Each bush provided about 30 artichokes each year for a total of 120 artichokes that all had to be harvested within a 2 month period. I had so many I gave a lot of them away to coworkers. I think if I ever eat another artichoke again, it will be too soon.

There was a semi-small 20'x10' garden area for annual vegetables and greens. In this area there were eggplants, tomatoes, romaine lettuce, cabbage, radishes, carrots, watermelon mushrooms and zucchini. A lot of zucchini and tomatoes were given away too since they grew in abundance so much I could not eat them all. And this was just the back yard.

The front yard had a lime tree, orange tree and cherry tree. The cherry tree became a sort of gathering place of the neighborhood because it grew so many. I loved when little children would come over and be completely amazed at the fact that cherries just magically grew off this tree and you could eat them right away. It was a learning experience for them given that they always thought cherries only grew in the store and cherries are a premium just about everywhere these days. They don't last more than a few days once picked so they rarely ever make it to the grocery store. I absolutely love cherries and was eating them every day for 2 weeks, even filling up one gallon Ziploc bags and bringing them to work. I left one in the break room once and it was gone within 2 hours when I went back to check on it. The memories that one cherry tree and the families and children that picked from it will always be with me.

Please note that there is one way to turn your liability house into an asset. This does not mean that it has to be rented out fully. If you have a spare room, you can rent it out or do AirBnb (my long term plan after some slight modifications). AirBnb is more beneficial in the fact that it can produce far more income in many areas than renting the room full time. This does not take into effect that you would constantly have to deal with another person or stranger living in your house. With AirBnb you can dictate when you want to be alone. This means that you can ensure that if you want some privacy, you can take down the listing on the website so the room can not be rented. If you do it right, renting a room can pay your property taxes, utilities and you will still have some money left over. In effect, this makes your house an asset while you are still living in it and do not have to turn it into a rental and deal with bad tenants.

CHAPTER 3

TRANSPORTATION

I worked hard, I deserve a brand new car! Uh, okay. Please keep in mind that a car is a huge depreciating asset. It's like buying a new couch. You can barely get rid of a used couch these days. Cars are turning into the same thing. I bought one new car at the age of 18 and it is the least loved cars of all the ones I have owned. At this point, I drive a 5 year old Toyota Corolla and am very happy with the gas mileage and rarity of maintenance given that it take synthetic oil and only needs to be changed once every 5,000 miles. And yes, I do my own oil changes.

I will always recommend buying a used vehicle. The best deals are typically from private owners that have cared for their cars over the years. The second best option is from a rental car company that is retiring their old fleet. Hertz has really nice cars that are always well maintained on the inside, outside as well as the engine. This will be the place I go for my next vehicle.

Maintaining your vehicle is definitely your responsibility. Since cars are depreciating assets, people often don't take care of them and if a large $1,000.00 repair bill comes around, many people will buy a new car instead of just paying the $1,000.00 to have it repaired. If you have a car with an ugly exterior that is dark and color, Armor All goes a long way. My mother had a maroon truck with horrible paint peeling on the hood but if you put Armor All on it once a week, it practically disappeared.

If you want to make an old, ugly car look new there are three things you can do. First of all, wash it and clean it inside and out. Make sure to wash the windows to a high-gloss shine without any streaks. The second thing is simply to meticulously clean the tires and add tire-wet. This simple 10 minute task makes the oldest of cars look 8 years newer. The third is to replace the headlight covers (not the headlight themselves). This option is a big more expensive but if your headlight covers turn into that undoubtedly milk white ugly color, replacing them will again, take away the look of 8 years of age by replacing them.

Maintain your vehicle regularly. Don't wait 8,000 miles for an oil change. If your car has a maintenance required signal, respond to it and get the oil changed. If you go to an oil change place and they promise that they offer other services here is a tip. Bring a tire pressure gauge with you. If they state they inflate your tires to the proper PSI and you have the gauge with you and it doesn't match after they are done, you have some wiggle room. This means they are cutting corners. I used to work in an oil change center and there were people that would do this. If the PSI didn't match, they would complain and say that we didn't deliver what was promised, I want a free....insert whatever here. I want a free Air Filter. I want a free vacuum of the full interior. I want a free window wash of all the windows. I want free windshield wipers. This is only if you are not afraid of complaining and asking for some sort of compensation or a way for the company to make up for it.

To keep your engine and brakes optimum condition, don't drive like a nutball. I'm not telling you to drive like Miss Daisy but don't step on the gas as fast as you possibly can to rev the engine. Don't drive 100 mph on the freeway. This breaks down your engine and wastes way too much gas. Don't slam the breaks constantly at the last second. You will not only look like a jerk to the people in front of you, but you also look like a jerk to any passengers you may have in the vehicle and will wear out your brakes very quickly. New brakes are expensive!

Keep your car as long as possible. Even if the transmission goes out which is the most expensive repair job anyone can deal with, consider getting the transmission repaired or replaced. $3,000.00 in repairs is still a great deal if you compare it to a new (to you) $10,000.00 car.

CHAPTER 4

CREDIT CARDS

Oh boy, this is a tough and serious one. Financial experts out there tell you not to use a credit card. I agree to an extent. My credit card is my auto-pay for all my utilities. It pays my cable bill, garbage, electricity, water and home improvements. However, I pay it off Bi-Weekly. That's right. Not monthly, but Bi-Weekly and it is not used for purchases like groceries at such. Why? Simply because using a credit cards is a gift to you by the credit card companies to help you spend an average of 17% more than you would if you were carrying cash instead. Credit card companies give you the gift of crazy interest fees, currently an average of 19%. Thank you so much Mr. Credit Card Company. I appreciate you helping to make me poor. Since I don't fly, Air miles are a terrible way to try and get my business. I much prefer cash back and gift cards. Why? Simple. These are my Christmas presents to family and friends. That's right. I don't buy Christmas presents because my credit card company buys them for me. This year I have enough for $250.00 in Home Depot gift cards AND $100.00 in Lowe's gift cards. The credit card companies get deals from these companies at a lower rate to offer their customers as "rewards". It is a win-win-win for the credit card company, the retailer and me.

If you do not have the discipline to pay off your credit card every month, do not use them. 70% of the population carries a balance. I do not subscribe to that type of culture. It is used very little and for very specific reasons, as it should be. But credit card companies make BILLIONS of dollars every year knowing full well that people are not very disciplined in this country, so they take full advantage. Don't let them take advantage of you.

If you are in the process of getting out of debt in terms of credit cards, I recommend calling the credit card company asking for a lower APR. They will say no, of course. This is when you ask for a supervisor. The supervisor is also trained to say no. Tell them that you have an offer from a different credit card for $0 transfer fees, available balance of $12,000.00 and that you are going to transfer your balance to their credit card if they do not lower their interest rate. They will now lower it around 2%-3%. This is when you say you want them to lower it by 5% or more. They will say no, tell them again that you are going to close your account and go with another credit card company. Call their bluff. They will go to 5%.

An additional option is to shop around for a credit card that offers $0 transfer fees and no interest for 12 months. If you have good credit, this will be easy to find. If you have any balances, transfer them to your new card that has no interest for a year. During that year, work aggressively to pay them off and CLOSE OUT YOUR OLD CARD. This will take away the temptation of continuing to use your old credit card and accumulating more debt.

CHAPTER 5

COLLEGE

Let me first say that I went to college. And I regret every day and every single dollar I spent on it. My mother made $6.00 too much in the previous tax year to get a scholarship so it was all on me. Over $20,000.00 in fact. I went, I got an education in computer technology with a minor in electronics. I graduated 2 months right after the dot com bubble burst. I never did get a job in my field and have had to take whatever I could get in terms of the job market ever since.

Let me throw some numbers at you. Only 27% of people get a job in their field of study. 85% of people hate their jobs. What does that tell you? That besides the rare few such as doctors and lawyers and such, college is a complete waste of money and time. I wasted years of my life to get that stupid degree. Years later the college I went to went bankrupt. Despite having a degree, it has done absolutely nothing for me.

Long gone are the 1970's where a degree was low cost, easy to obtain and would get you a job very quickly once you graduated. Sorry to say it, but I do not believe in college.

Many parents will create college savings plans for their kids with the notion that in doing so, they will help ensure their child's future. But if it doesn't work for 83% of the population, and 85% of the people hate their jobs, why are you putting your child through this? The average cost of a 4 year degree (AVERAGE COST) is nearing $24,000.00. I would tell your children that as soon as they graduate high school, they need to get a full-time job. Every penny has to go to you (the parent). They get $100.00 per week to spend on whatever and you save everything they make for 4 years. Let's say they make an average of $25,000.00 per year and bring home $20,000.00. This is a very low estimate, so it is very feasible. Save that money for 4 years for a total of $80,000.00. Add your saved $24,000.00 and you have $104,000.00. By the way, $104,000.00 will buy a lot of house. Don't think of places like Manhattan or the San Francisco Bay Area. Think outside the box on where to buy and don't completely disregard foreclosures. Buy your kid a $104,000.00 house! If they graduate at the age of 17 and follow this plan, they will have a full-paid off house by the age of 21. By the time they are legally able to drink, they will have a paid off home. Think about this long and hard and decide what is right for your child. A life of debt or a life of not only financial freedom, but a life where they can CHOOSE what they want to do, when they want to work, how much they want to work and so on.

CHAPTER 6

LAUNDRY

Laundry has always been one of my favorite frugal topics. It seems like when people are at the end of their rope, don't know where to turn to and refuse to change their lifestyle, they look at the miniscule cost of laundry. I don't get it either but it is still fun to talk about.

Let's say your favorite brand is Tide at $17.00 per bottle that does 64 loads. Isn't it funny how those 64 loads seem to last only a couple weeks. Yeah, there is a reason for that. When people do laundry, they typically fill the cap, dump it in and start the washer. Well, did you EVER read the instructions? No, seriously…did you? You know you're not supposed to use a full cap, right? But so many people do, using up to 5x too much laundry soap. The instructions typically read something like this:

Measure with cap. For medium loads, fill to bar 1. For large loads, fill to bar 3. For HE full loads, fill to bar 5. Add clothes, start washer.

So what line are you filling your cap to? Go ahead, I'll wait. Uh-huh.

There are a lot of ways to save costs on laundry soap. Almost all stores have store brand laundry detergent purposefully intended to mimic or match the brand name product. So for half the price, you can get a laundry detergent that smells just as good and washes just as well as Tide.

Let's take it another step. There are brands in the Hispanic section that sell for about $3.00 and wash 32 loads. A big bargain. These are typically the dry powder laundry soap, but did you know….

The majority of liquid laundry detergent is made of water? Yup. It sure is. You can easily make your own with the following recipe:

1 bar of grated Fels Naptha or Zote soap (some people even use Ivory bath soap)

1 cup of washing soda (not baking soda)

1 cup of Borax

Put these ingredients in a 5 gallon bucket and add boiling hot water. Leave overnight and stir in the morning. You now have 5 GALLONS of laundry soap for the cost of about $2.00. If you were to dispense this into those left over Tide bottles, it would amount to about 12 cents a bottle.

I used to notice when using the expensive stuff that my dark clothes that were black would often start getting more and more light in color. I found out this was due to the bleaching agents found in most detergents so I started making my own. I have now taken it yet another step further.

For stains, I will rub a Fels Naptha or Zote bar on the stain and attempt to get it out with water. I then throw in all my laundry in the washing machine. That's right. I barely ever even use ANY laundry soap these days. I don't work at a dirty job and very rarely get so dirty I would even need soap. So why bother paying for it? The agitation cycle in the washing machine does most of the cleaning anyway. It's like when you see those videos with people beating their clothes on rocks to wash them without the use of soap. Many countries don't use soap in their laundry and their clothing is still in great shape. Soap pollutes our waterways, has ingredients nobody can even pronounce and is pretty much useless unless you are trying to slowly bleach your clothes. So slowly ween yourself off of a huge amount of soap and save your family a ton of money.

Line dry your clothes. I know, I know...it's too much hassle. You don't like the way they are stiff and itchy. Well, let me throw some logic at you. We all know that dryers cost money to run. They cost a LOT of money to buy, which is beyond me. If you line dry your clothes and leave them out for 2 days, they magically become soft again and there is no stiffness. If you don't have time for this but still want to save some money you can line dry them, then put them in the dryer for 10-15 minutes on the fluff cycle to get rid of the stiffness.

If you still want to use your dryer you can still save a little money doing different things. When doing a load in the dryer, add an already dried towel to the load. This will decrease the drying time by about 20 minutes. I also recommend using the low-heat setting. Your clothes get dry just as fast but it helps get rid of static, if that is an issue for you.

CHAPTER 7

CLOTHING

Oh boy, this is a sensitive topic. Everyone wants to look better than everyone else so they can stand out from the crowd and find a mate, right?

Back in the early 1900's, children did not have shoes. They went to school barefoot. Typically, children would have 3 sets of clothes. 1 for school, 1 for chores after school and 1 for church (maybe with shoes, but mostly not). Now our closets are filled to the brim. We open the door, see 2 dozen jackets and hoodies, along with our dresser that has 20 pairs of pants and 30 shirts and we sit there staring at the inside abundance of freshly cleaned and folded clothing thinking "I have nothing to wear". Crazy how times have changed, isn't it?

Let me provide this little tidbit of advice. Never, I repeat never ever purchase clothing online without seeing it in person first. If you know exactly what you are looking for, that's great. If not, DO NOT BUY IT. 100% of the time these purchases typically end up being a complete waste of money where the item doesn't fit properly, is not true to size or the color looks awful with our skin color. So just stop and don't bother with that option.

Before shopping for clothing anywhere, put the word out that you want/need new clothing or jewelry (or whatever). Post it on Facebook or Twitter or Instagram or whatever app you kids are into these days. Most times people will be more than happy to give you their old clothes or jewelry that they are no longer using. They get to get rid of it without feeling bad because it will go to someone they know that will use and appreciate it. I have paid it forward and given my clothes and accessories to others when I could no longer use them.

Thrift stores are an amazing thing, but it now depends greatly on your location. In California, a pair of jeans at a thrift store was $16.00. It cost the same to buy a brand new pair at Walmart as it did to shop at the thrift store in California. Now, designer jeans at a thrift store where I live in Arizona are 2 for $5.00. That's a deal I can live with. Previously, I would only purchase a pair of pants to replace a pair that had worn out or my size changed and needed to be replaced. I only had 3 pairs of pants. 1 pair of jeans, 1 grey dress pants and 1 black dress pants. Can you guess which two were designated for work? And please note that I always wear pants 2-3 times before washing in the lower temperature months. This saves immensely on electric and water costs but we will get to that later.

Shirts are typically anywhere from $12-$50 at a retail store. I have not purchased a shirt at a typical retail store as long as I can remember in my adult life. All my shirts were purchased at thrift stores at an average of $2.00 each.

Be sure to choose clothing that suits your body style. We all are great at hiding the ugly and should keep to those rules when shopping at thrift stores. Try on everything before you go through with a purchase. V-necks and jeans are my every day style. During the winter, it is typically jeans and a shirt or sweater with a stylish scarf and a blazer.

You can buy just about anything at a thrift store. Jeans, dress pants (cheaper than jeans at all thrift stores), t-shirts, v-necks, office wear, shoes, socks, bras. I purchase everything there except the occasional pair of shoes and underwear. The last time I purchased shoes was about 3 years ago.

It is very important to keep your clothing in good condition so they will last longer. Make sure you have extra shoe laces and shoe polish. My adidas shoes are at least 7 years old but look brand new just because of shoelaces and shoe polish. Do not neglect your shoes. It took you time to earn the money to pay for them and they take care of your feet, which in turn can take care of your posture and assist with physical fitness. Of all items, shoes should be getting the most attention and upkeep.

When you look at other people, how often do you notice what they are wearing? Unless they are dirty from working a specific job or extremely unfashionable or something, you don't really notice much. If you do, it is likely only a 2 second thought then you get to know the person underneath. As a woman, I find that as long as my makeup is done well and my hair looks well kept, the clothing goes mostly unnoticed. Your perceived fitness level (are you overweight, do you carry yourself well, do you have confidence, etc.) Solid colors without modern fads is the easiest and cheapest way to go.

If you do purchase your clothing at a typical retailer, be sure to try them on first to ensure proper fit and that they "cover the ugly" to your satisfaction before proceeding with a purchase.

CHAPTER 8

MAKEUP & HAIR DYE

Yes, I purchase the majority of my makeup at the Dollar Tree. Many are name brands like Loreal and CoverUp. Mascara and eyeliner are the easiest. Black and black is all you need, no matter your eye color.

Foundation is also purchased at the Dollar Tree. The majority of foundations these days do not have to be an exact match to your skin color, but should come close. If you have a good powder to go over the foundation, you should be fine. I do purchase my powder at full price at Walmart for about $7.50 which lasts about 3-4 months at a time. TrueMatch is what I use. With the foundation, you can add water to make it last longer in small amounts. It may extend it for a couple weeks if you add to it regularly in small amounts so it mixes well.

Eye shadow and blush are not used. I was always taught that makeup should look as natural as possible, and these two options seemed to make me look more like a plastic Barbie Doll than a natural look. And they were big in the 80's, why is it still a thing now? I just don't understand these options I suppose.

Lipstick is also a full-price item that I buy for about $2.50 at Walmart. It is called Wet N'Wild and I believe (but am not sure) that this is their store brand. Remember, the lighter the lipstick color the younger it makes you look. The darker the color the lipstick, the older it makes you look. I am not saying to go to the lightest color they have but if you are on the middle age or slightly older (under age 55), stick with light colors to help make yourself look younger.

For hair dye, I will use whatever I find wherever I am. For instance, if I am at the Dollar Tree and they have it in a really light blonde color, I'll use it. If I am at Walmart and they have a light blonde color, I will buy that. It is such a small purchase and lasts for months at a time, so I don't spend a lot of time "shopping" for this type of item. In between dyes if I am low on money, I will squeeze a lemon on top of my head to naturally lighten the roots. I still have yet to determine if this method even works.

CHAPTER 9

CLEANING PRODUCTS

What can I say, I don't use much and add water to everything.

Toilets are cleaned with bleach and a toilet brush once every few days. That's it. And my toilets are gleaming white.

Vinegar is added to a spray bottle, about 1/4 vinegar and 3/4 water. I have every essential oil on earth purchased years ago. It lasts forever (literally) so I will add a few drops into the bottle if I don't want to smell vinegar when I clean. Please note that if you use vinegar for cleaning, the smell dissipates after a few minutes. This mix is used for countertops, dusting all surfaces and washing windows. This is also very good at getting rid of calcium deposits on silver colored hardware, including kitchen cabinet hardware, shower heads or faucets.

I very rarely use paper towels. These are mostly just to wash the windows on my car so they are streak free. For 99% of the projects, I just cut up old shirts into squares and leave them in a little box under the kitchen sink and use them to clean. They go in the wash with all my other laundry. These are used to wash the interior and exterior of my car too (not including windows).

Comet or Barkeeper's Friend are used for bathtubs, showers and sinks along with a standard sponge. They only cost about $1.00 and last for months.

For flooring, I use a Libman. It's sort of like a Swiffer except the spray option is not battery operated, but operated by hand. You can use whatever liquid you want in a refillable reservoir and the cleaning pad on the bottom does not have to be replaced. It is attached with Velcro and can be taken off anytime and thrown into your laundry for cleaning. It's like a Swiffer where you never have to buy anything to "re-fill" since you can do it yourself.

When it comes to dish soap, buy whichever one you like since this is not an exorbitant cost. Now, add water to it. Most dish soap is super concentrated and you are supposed to add water anyway. Of course, most people don't read this part of the label. Start with 10% water. Then add another 10% water. Once you get to the point you are comfortable with, stay there. Be sure to buy dish soap in bulk because the more you buy, the less you pay long term with this product.

CHAPTER 10

FOOD

How much do you spend every month on food? Go ahead and check out your last receipt. I'll wait. Okay, great. If you are the average American family, you spend about $2,667.00 per year at food at home.

This is $222.25 per month.

Now, how much did you spend on eating out? If you are the average American family, you spent $3,935.00.

This is $327.91 per month.

Learning to cook at home, and cooking all of your meals at home is the fastest possible way to start saving money on food. If you don't know how to cook, don't be embarrassed. As time passes on, less and less young people are learning to cook on their own. Just ask a friend or relative if they can teach you. There are also plenty of youtube videos available. We all had to learn to boil water at some point, right? Then it moved on to scrambled eggs and toast, and so on. Never be embarrassed to learn a new skill, even if it seems like an embarrassment.

Now that we have figured out your costs, it's time to get to business. How much did you spend on drinks? How much of that bill was soda? How much were your Arizona Iced Teas? Gatorade? The average PERSON (not family) spends about $850.00 per year on SODA. That's about $70.00 per person on drinks, which is ridiculous, extremely unhealthy and insane.

After years of personal research, I have dwindled down my food bill to $60-$100 per month which includes everything. Every morsel of food, every drink, eating out and all you can imagine. Here's how.

First of all, I want to talk about breakfast food and cereals. When people think of breakfast, they might think of bacon, eggs and pancakes drizzled in maple or butter flavored syrup. Some might think of hash browns, eggs and sausage. Some might think of cereal like Lucky Charms, Frosted Mini Wheats and so on.

So here is something very important that I learned years ago. Cereal is just sugar. That is literally all it is. Those little marshmallows are made of sugar. The "wheat" that is not really wheat anymore is made of unhealthy sugar carbs. They are packed with calories and no nutrition. What does nutrition have to do with it if it tastes good? I will tell you. Things like cereal does not digest well and makes you hungry only a half an hour later. Have you ever read what a true serving size of cereal is and only eaten the serving size? Of course not. You fill the bowl to the brim and cover it in milk. You typically eat 4-5 servings or more in a single bowl and you are STILL hungry an hour later. That is what I mean when I talk about nutrition. So I started making my own cereal. Here is how:

I buy a 25 lbs. bag of organic oatmeal for $23.00 which lasts about a year and a half.

I buy 10 lbs. of banana chips (not bananas, but banana chips) in bulk for about $20.00 which lasts a year and a half.

I buy 15 lbs. of organic sugar free flavored granola for about $40.00.

This makes my breakfast for a year and a half for a total cost of $83.00. I have eaten the same breakfast for about 4 years at this point. The oats are slow-burning carbs that have more fiber and natural ingredients than cereal which helps with energy levels, appetite suppressant and digestion. The rest is full of potassium and flavor.

Drinks:

I won't pretend that I drink only water. I drink a couple other things as well, but never soda. I have not purchased soda in several years.

Coffee is my addiction and I used to love Starbuck's and the Baskin Robbins Mocha Blast. However, I learned I could make my own EVERYTHING for pennies. The cost of these drinks at Baskin Robbins or Starbucks became so expensive, I was backed into a corner and FORCED to learn to make them myself.

So, I bought a Mr. Coffee Espresso maker at a thrift store for $4.00 and have been using it ever since. It makes latte's for me in the winter and frozen coffee drinks in the summer.

Latte's are just espresso and frothed milk with a little sweetener. I use 1 teaspoon of sugar with each drink, and typically drink 2-4 drinks per day.

The iced coffee recipe is as follows:

Make yourself 4 cups of espresso using the espresso machine. Once done, put in the refrigerator overnight to chill.

In the morning, add the espresso and milk together just as you normally would with a latte, except put it in a blender.

Add 1 teaspoon sugar and 1 teaspoon of Hershey's sugar free chocolate syrup.

Add 6-10 ice cubes (depends on your preference of how icy it is) and turn on the grate function for 1 minute.

Instant Starbuck's Frappuccino.

As a second, more expensive option try DaVinci Mocha Frappe Freeze Coffee Mix. You can get them at Smart and Final or online. These are more expensive and much higher in sugar, but are even MORE delicious than any Starbuck's I have ever had. A #10 can is about $6.00 and makes 27 servings. 27 servings versus the 1 serving you would get for $6.00 at Starbuck's is insane. If you decide to go with this option, add 12 ice cubes, 3 scoops of the powder and 1 cup of milk to a blender on the grate option for 1 minute. I promise this will be the best coffee drink you have ever had and you will never go back to Starbuck's again for a daily Frappuccino. Also, when you do it, adding the 12 ice cubes in the blender, it doubles the amount. So, it really makes 2 servings per 3 scoops instead of 1 shown on the label. An additional savings and a real treat.

Instead of sodas, make homemade lemon water. If you like sugar...it's bad for you, but add sugar and make your own lemonade. I have seen people make weird mint/cucumber concoctions and such. This is not for me but to each his own.

Instead of buying that Arizona Iced Tea for $2.50 every day, buy a packet of tea for $2.50 and make yourself 50 of them. Put in water, lay in the sun all day and you instantly have your own Iced Tea but without all the preservatives and unnatural flavorings.

COUNTING CALORIES

A moment must be taken to advise everyone that there is an obesity epidemic in America. This is partly due to now living sedentary lives working in cubicles for the majority of the US population. Processed and pre-packaged foods as well as non-nutritional drinks certainly play a huge part. As I write this, I am a 38 year old female, 5'7 and 142 lbs. The average woman my age is 5'4 and 164 lbs. So I am taller and thinner. I am not tooting my own horn but offering a word of advice about "counting calories".

I have eaten the same breakfast every day for 4 years that is heart healthy, high in fiber and potassium made of slow burning carbs and is sugar free. It consists of about 300 calories so I don't have to count this every day as a different food and calorie count since it is always the same.

However, the calories included in my coffee drinks does not go unnoticed. This is why I only eat twice a day (at most) and sometimes only once. The breakfast can often times keep me full all day when not being highly active. While coffee is a calorie-free drink, the milk that is included in the drinks is not. One cup of milk, which is typically what the coffee requires has about 100-120 calories. If I am drinking 2 of these drinks, that is 240 calories. If I drink 4 of these drinks in a day, that is 480 calories. Breakfast is about 300 calories. So with only breakfast and coffee, this can make up 780 calories in a day without including dinner. Simplifying things makes it so I only have to worry about cooking 1 meal a day (dinner), at only 300-500 calories, which is a very satisfying meal.

While most meals at restaurants contain 1500 calories, this is more than my daily intake and I can not eat out anymore. I am so accustomed to eating such a healthy diet that eating at a restaurant now makes me sick and clogs up my digestion for 3 days at a time.

MEAT

As the summer of 2020 is in full swing, and the current issues with the Coronavirus, prices of meat in the stores has absolutely skyrocketed to insane levels. I never thought I would see such a spike in my life. But I have and so have you. It is time to think outside of the box when it comes to the amount of meat you eat and how you obtain it.

First of all, people think they need meat for protein. Let me educate you a little bit on protein. I am not a doctor or a nutritionist but I am a professional label reader, and have been for 10+ years. Protein is in everything. It is in oatmeal, leafy greens, spinach, beans, soy, tofu. So please don't think that meat is your ONLY option for protein.

56 grams of protein is recommended for the average sedentary man. 46 grams of protein is recommended for the average sedentary woman. What does that mean? It means if you close your fist, it should be the size of your fist. Men's fists will be larger than a woman's, so you get the idea. Instead of slabbing a pound of meat on a plate next to your instant mashed potatoes and 2 green beans, think this through. You only NEED meat the size of the back of your fist. Or do you? What else did you eat that day that might have had protein in it? Did you eat scrambled eggs and bacon for breakfast? Then you probably don't need any meat with your dinner. You might need a lot less.

Here is a trick with chicken breasts. Chickens are typically provided hormones to make them grow like crazy so they can be "harvested" faster. This also makes their breasts extremely large and thick. So when you are cooking straight chicken breasts, turn 1 into 2. Cut the chicken breast long-ways. Serve half to yourself and save the rest for tomorrow, or share it with your husband, or kid, or dog, or whatever. The point is that cutting the breast in half long ways makes 1 breast turn into 2 and if you are the cook and someone else is eating half, they won't even notice that it was cut in half.

Here is a trick with steak to make it look bigger and go further. Once you have cooked the steak, slice it into thin slices. Then slight space the slices apart and tilt them over. This will make a small-fist sized piece of stake look twice as big when done correctly. People have a tendency to eat everything on their plate. Our parents taught us that if we don't eat everything on our plate, it is wasting food. So a natural action is to eat it all.

FISH

Fish is probably the meat with the most potential. I will explain why. It is still legal, and not much of a hassle to go fishing and catch your own food these days. If you like and eat a lot of fish, pay the $40-ish for a fishing license and spend a few hours on your weekend catching your own food and spending time with your children. If you catch 1 fish per month you have already tripled your money. If you catch 1 fish per fishing trip and go 4 times per month, well you get the idea. Fish are easy to clean, easy to catch and easy to cook. They are very healthy when eaten in moderation from a clean water source.

If you live near the ocean, you might not even need a fishing license if you are fishing from a pier. This is amazing because you can also crab fish from a pier for free without a license and can collect mussels and such during the right tides. Foraging and fishing at the ocean is one of the things I will miss most about living near the coast in California. Abundant wildlife that can practically just be picked up and eaten for free.

FRUIT

Different fruits cost different things at different times of the year. Most citrus fruits are cheapest around Christmas time and in the summer. Apples and oranges are typically the cheapest. These are high in fiber and just plain delicious

## VEGETABLES

I categorize vegetables into three different categories. Vegetables, root vegetables and Leafy Greens.

Vegetables are things like green beans, zucchini and such. Root vegetables are things like potatoes and carrots. Leafy Greens are lettuces.

The cheapest vegetables you can get are root vegetables. Potatoes, sweet potatoes and carrots are by far the cheapest. Make sure to get your carrots uncut. Buying pre-cut carrots quadruples the price.

If you purchase your vegetables in pre-weighed bags. For instance, 2 lbs. of carrots. Take those bags to the weighing scale. When these are packaged, the manufacturer must provide the minimum weight of 2 lbs. This means that there can be a bag full of 3 lbs. of carrots in a 2 lbs. bag but you only get charged for 2 lbs. Don't believe me? Test it. Weigh a couple of bags next time you are in the store and you will see that some have big differences in weight. Same goes for potatoes. Take a couple of those 5 lbs. bags and you might be able to get 6 lbs. worth of potatoes for the cost of a 5 lbs. bag.

For the most part, you get the best bang for your buck with green vegetables by buying them frozen. Don't think that they are not as fresh. While the "fresh" green vegetables are rotting on the shelves in the vegetable section, the frozen ones were flash frozen right after picking when they were at their freshest point. A bonus is that they have a longer shelf life in your home if you purchase them frozen. So if you are the type that buys fresh vegetables with good intentions but they keep going bad, buy your broccoli in the frozen food aisle.

Leafy greens. So here is the deal, I do not like salads and I do not believe in them. Whaaaa? Don't get me wrong, leafy greens have tons of vitamins and minerals but salads have almost zero calories. A full head of lettuce has only about 50 calories. When you eat a salad, you are getting most of the calories from the added things like bacon bits, sunflower seeds, cranberries and sugar coated dressing. That is correct. Most of the calories come from the dressing. So how do I eat my leafy greens? I eat them in stir-fry's fully cooked. They add a little bit of flavor but not much but you do get the essential vitamins and minerals when you cook them with your other things. If you or your kids hate leafy greens, this is the way to go.

If you can afford it, buy organic potatoes and sweet potatoes. Recently, I saw organic potatoes and sweet potatoes for 69 cents per pound. Why go organic with these? Because non-organic potatoes are sprayed with a growth inhibitor so the eyes of the potatoes won't grow before they are purchased at the store. Organic ones are not sprayed.

This means that you can cut up your organic potato for frying and cut off a small piece or eye. Dump that in your garden or just dig a little hole and put it in. In the spring, you might end up with a free crop of potatoes just by doing this.

CHAPTER 11

YOU CAN DITCH THE COW AND MEAT ALL-TOGETHER MAKE YOUR OWN MILK AND PROTEIN

I make my own oat milk and soy milk. Both are extremely easy and will save a ton of money if you and your family are big milk drinkers. The soy beans are purchased in bulk once a year for about $35.00. You can get them at Costco or Winco if you live in the western United States. Same with the oats as indicated. These bulk purchases will last me a year at minimum. $35.00 for a year's worth of oat milk and breakfast? That is correct. Here are the recipes:

Oat Milk:

4 cups of ice cold water

1 cup of Old Fashioned Rolled Oats (make sure it is

1 tbsp honey or sweetener. You can use vanilla extract or sugar if you prefer

Blend 20-30 seconds in blender

Drain through nut milk bag (not strainer or cheesecloth)

Strain a 2nd time if needed but it is not likely

Store in refrigerator, will last 5-7 days


Soy Milk

Soak ½ cup (yellow) Soybeans overnight

Drain the soybeans and remove the exterior of the bean

Add to blender with 3 cups of water

Blend for about 30 seconds

Drain the mixture with a cheesecloth

Put milk in saucepan and bring to a boil

Cook over medium heat for 20 minutes, stirring occasionally

Add sweetener such as vanilla extract, sugar, or dates to your liking. Re-blend if necessary

Lasts about 5 days in refrigerator.


TOFU


The meat alternative. For this recipe, you will need a tofu press and coagulant. You can make tofu using your already home made soy milk. It can be fried, added to stews or soups and is very high in protein. Asian countries have tofu as a main staple in their diet and those that live to be over 100 years old swear by it. I would recommend looking up videos on youtube for this option since it is difficult to explain without seeing it being made.

Given that food is one of the biggest and fastest places to save money, I have listed the main components of my food saving tactics below:

*Eat less meat. Cut the meat so that it LOOKS like more, but is half of what you are used to

*Make your own meat alternative (tofu)

*Stop drinking soda

*Make your own flavored drinks

*Fish for your dinner if you can by getting and using a fishing license

*Eat fruit and vegetables in season

*Weight your bagged vegetables to get the highest amount for lowest cost

*Purchase frozen vegetables if you have good intentions but might not get to it before it goes bad

*Make your own cereal and buy in bulk

*Make your own soy milk and oat milk and stop buying cow milk


CHAPTER 12

ENTERTAINMENT


So let's start with the basics. Cable TV seems to be the main staple for anyone seeking entertainment. But who wants to pay $150 a month to watch TV? When I was a kid it was $30 a month and that was considered expensive. Extra packages, extra channels for only an additional $20 a month seems ridiculous. I don't care how entertaining the channels are. If you have to work 10 hours a month just to pay for cable TV, they are asking too much and ripping off their clientele.

When people think of cutting the cable there is an anxiety that seems to take over. They worry about their sports packages and movie nights and oh no, what will the children do!?! An antenna seems to be the solution, right? Wrong. While an antenna will get you a few major networks depending on your location, the options are minimal. CBS, ABC, Fox and maybe PBS along with some channels that speak a language unknown to you.

Let me break it down for you. If you have internet, you have unlimited options. I will explain. I have a Roku box purchased for $30.00. This is about the same price as an antenna that you would affix to your roof. This $30.00 Roku box which was a one-time cost saves me so much money.

A Roku Box offers FREE apps such as The Roku Channel, The NFL Network, Crackle, The CW Channel, ABC, NBC, CBS, Filmrise, Tubi, Freeflix, Fawesome, Stirr, Pluto and Xumo. Those apps might not sound like much but lets go into it a little bit.

When you click on the app for Pluto TV you get tons of kids channels, ABS, Fox, NBC, CBS, PBS and about 150 more channels that are completely free.

When you click on the Crackle app, you open it up to THOUSANDS of free movies. Most you have never heard of and it is fun to watch B movies that were not blockbusters. It adds diversity to your style of watching. However, there are blockbusters in there as well.

The CW Channel is exactly what it sounds like. It is all television shows that are on CW. Right now that includes The 100, Riverdale, Stargirl, Nancy Drew, Batwoman, DC's Legends of Tomorrow, In The Dark, The Flash, Bulletproof and so on.

Tubi, Freeflix, Fawesome, Stuirr and Xumo all include free movies and TV. Channels upon channels that you have never even heard of and many that you have. One of my favorite channels is the History Channel, and even this channel is found on two of these free app options.

If you want Live Cable TV but don't want to pay $150 or more, I highly recommend Sling TV. For $30 a month you can get live TV with the top rated networks like FX, AMC, The History Channel, FXX, MSNBC, TNT, TBS, TruTV, USA, SyFy, Comedy Central and so on. Another option is Philo TV for $20.00 a month. They have different channels, but are also Live TV.

Comcast, Coxx Communications, AT&T and most cable companies are extremely overpriced and losing business quickly to these free options. While an antenna is an option, it is no longer the best one.

HANGING OUT WITH FRIENDS

So who says you have to meet up with friends and go to the bar, bowling, dinner or a movie? These options are all very pricey and are a distraction from having real conversations with your friends.

I have always advocated home BBQ's. These are my fondest memories as a child. Family or friends of my Mom would come over and she would put some hot dogs on the grill. Add some potato salad, corn on the cob and drinks with some background music on the radio and you have yourself an intimate little gathering without all the typical background noise you would get elsewhere. That's not to mention when you are finally able to drown out the background noise and your best friend is telling you the most intimate details of her divorce while pouring her heart out, and all of a sudden the waitress comes up and asks if you would like a refill. Or the disco lights and music at the bowling alley are hurting your eyes and ears so much that you can't make out a word she is saying.

If you have children, a sprinkler and cheap Slip-N-Slide will keep them entertained for hours. This is one of my favorite memories growing up. Ever hear of Body Bubbles? These are Inflatable

Balls that you put on your kids and they run around and bump into each other as hard as they can trying to knock each other down but they never get hurt. These are a ton of fun too. One time cost will last a good 5 years of BBQ's for the kids to stay entertained all day.

I find it odd that people will drive to a coffee shop and have someone make their drink for $5.00 or more every day. I have to wonder what is at the root of this masterful marketing scheme. Is it the feeling of luxury because someone else is making your drink? Is it the social interaction with the cashier? I don't get it. Just make your own coffee and go to a walking trail and sit on the bench. You will get the same people-watching effect as sitting in a booth inside of a purposefully darkened coffee shop.

## GET RE-ACQUAINTED WITH THE OUTDOORS

When was the last time you went hiking with friends? It has probably been a while. Maybe it's time to give them a call and go for a hike. Not a trail walk, a real hike. Pick a peak and go for it. Pack a couple sandwiches and granola bars and that is some free fun.

How about a picnic in the park feeding ducks and a frisbee or football? Don't bring bread, it is not good for ducks so try oatmeal instead. However, these provide tons of entertainment. There are usually benches located near duck ponds. When I was a kid my mom would go and sit on the bench while me and my brother would go hunting for eggs. We never, ever found any eggs because the parks and ponds were cleaned up daily from city maintenance. Mom knew that, but we didn't. We would look for hours. If we got tired of doing that, we would hunt for feathers to make our own pillows but by the time we filled our pockets they would all fly out by the time Mom was ready to go home.

## THE LIBRARY

The library is full of never-ending knowledge and entertainment. I think of libraries and computers of the Library of Alexandria for today. Books are never ending. In some instances, you can order online or from different libraries and your local library will email or text you when they are ready for pick up. New Release DVD's and Blu Ray's are heavily stocked.

The library has activities too. Sometimes they have craft night for the kids, or workshops depending on what you are interested in. Maybe it is crafts. Someone that wrote a book might live in the area and visit your library and teach people how to crochet. There might even be a money saving workshop coming near you!

Speaking of workshops, call your local Home Depot to see what workshops they have coming up. These are completely free of charge. I should know. I used to work there. Some are for adults to teach you about tiling, plumbing or fence building.

However, many Home Depot classes are for little kids. They might teach them how to build a mail box or bird box using scrap wood. A lot of times, Home Depot will even give them a little yellow apron just like the ones they were. They are just like the adult ones, only small for little kids. They love this. It is free entertainment, but it also might grow into a productive hobby for your kids.

If you live in a state that has redemption value for cans and bottles, have your kid(s) pick them up and teach them how money works. They spend a couple hours cleaning up a park full of cans and bottles. You take the kids along with you to the recycling center to teach them how garbage can be turned into money. You then give them the money and take them to the store where they get to use their money to buy whatever toy or candy they want. I can guarantee you that this will get them hooked on making money. They will be asking you to take them to the park all the time. Hey, no problem. You can read a book on the bench that you got from the library while your kids run around picking up cans and bottles. Repeat the process. Who knows, your kid might get rich this way.

BALLS AND GAMES

The cheapest ways to entertain yourself are with sports balls and games. These are items that have a one-time cost and re-pay you over and over and over again. You can use a ball hundreds or even thousands of times before it is time to replace. The best part is that you can get tons of sports equipment as well as board games at just about any thrift store. Footballs, Volleyballs, Baseballs, Softballs, Tennis Balls, Basketballs and so on. Also, the board games and puzzles available are not just weird games with missing pieces. When I visit a thrift store, I often see a lot of classics with all pieces included. Some examples are Yahtzee, Scrabble, Monopoly, Sorry and so on. And who knows, maybe you can try a new game that you have never seen before and find hours upon hours of new entertainment that you didn't even know existed. Many card games are available that you can use like simple decks of cards to play Go Fish or Poker. Other card decks are very inexpensive at a regular store like Uno (my favorite).

Since first being frugal with board games, balls and games, I have upgraded a bit. I now like to metal detect. Not only does this provide hours of entertainment and adventure, but I actually get something out of it. Gold, silver, rings, coins, necklaces, fish hooks. These things are found on the regular and I will eventually sell them for a huge profit. More than enough to pay for the initial cost of the metal detector and MAKE some money in the process.

CHAPTER 13

HYGIENE AND PERSONAL CARE

How is that $8.00 shampoo working out for you? How about the $12.00 conditioner, the $14.00 leave-in treatment and $18.00 scented body lotion? It might be burning a hole in your pocket.

I used to be one of those people too. I used to buy Infusium 23 for $5.00 for shampoo, $5.00 for conditioner and $5.00 for the leave in treatment. This was over 15 years ago at that high price. I used to buy the $18.00 bottle of lotion from Victoria's Secret along with about $120.00 per month on perfume and cologne. Well, that is long gone now.

Shampoo and conditioner are V05 for 87 cents each found on the very bottom shelf at Walmart. Lotion is the store brand, unscented which is usually around $3.00 and lasts for 6-8 months.

When it comes to dental care, please do not neglect your teeth and gums. Doing so can lead to periodontal disease, tooth extractions, expensive dental issues and can even lead to heart disease. Floss every day before brushing your teeth before bed.

As for the toothpaste itself, I see a lot of options out there for $5 or $6.00. The main ingredient for all toothpastes is fluoride and just about all of them use the same amount of this ingredient. What does that mean? It means that the extra $4.00 you are spending for the whitening option likely aren't really doing anything more than the cheapest option on the shelf. Here's what you should do next time you are buying toothpaste somewhere other than the dollar store. Look on the very bottom shelf. Scam across and look for the cheapest option. These are usually Aquafresh, Colgate and Ultrabrite. I have been using all 3 options for years and have not had a cavity since I was a young teenager. The flavors will all be different. Pick the one you like, but pick the cheapest option.

As for mouthwash, this is a luxury and not really a requirement for most people. However, if it is something that you like to use, go with the store brand for half the price of regular mouthwash. Take it a step further and use it a few times. Once you have, add 10% water to the mouthwash to dilute it a little bit. This will save you an additional 10% off the cheapest mouthwash option. You can always take it further and add more to save 20%, 30% and so on. Just start with adding 10% water and see how you like it, then move forward from there.

If you are concerned about the whitening agent in your toothpaste, this is always hydrogen peroxide and/or baking soda. Go buy some cheap hydrogen peroxide and baking soda (and maybe some peppermint oil) and it will last 3 years or more. Just sprinkle some baking soda or hydrogen peroxide on top of your toothpaste and see if it really makes a difference. You can also forego the toothpaste all together and brush with only the baking soda, peroxide and some peppermint oil.


CHAPTER 14

ELECTRICITY

There are so many ways you can save on electricity. My electric bill has been $40.00 or less per month for the majority of my adult life. I had two bills that exceeded that amount, and I lived in California where the electricity was 12 cents per kwh, far higher than the national average.


First things first. Replace any incandescent or CFL bulbs with LCD bulbs. I prefer the daylight bulbs that have a natural hue, but if you like the yellow hue, go for it. Remember that not all LCD bulbs are equal. Some use 23 watts, some use 15 watts, some use 11 and so on. I have found that the 9 watt LED bulbs are very bright. So bright that sometimes I have to unscrew a couple if there are 3 or 4 bulbs on a ceiling fan. Replace ALL light bulbs in your house. The cost of these keeps going down but I have found that Home Depot has the best prices for multi-packs. Typically these are packs of 12 bulbs.


Second. Put your TV, Computer, lamps or anything that has a plug on a power strip. No big deal. When you are not using it, turn it off at the power strip. Everyone has power strips sitting around in junk drawers but if you don't, they cost around $5.00. You will make your money back in the first month if you use it as intended, I promise.


I am not advocating getting rid of your appliances in order to upgrade them if they are still in working order. However, if you are in the market for a new TV, refrigerator or dishwasher, go as energy efficient as you can afford. My Vizio 52" LCD energy efficient TV uses only 50 watts and runs on my solar. My refrigerator is much smaller than the usual refrigerator and is only 11.1 cu. ft. It also runs on solar. These are my two biggest energy users in the home, aside from air conditioning in the summer. My last electric bill in the middle of July in the Mohave Desert was $43.00, which includes a $20.00 transmission fee. So in effect, I only used $23.00 worth of electricity to run the air conditioners and keep the home comfortable in the middle of the summer in the desert.

Use curtains and blinds as intended. Open them during the day for natural light and close them at night for privacy. Instead of flicking the switch whenever you walk into a room, remember that the windows are open and the sun is giving you brightness for free and you don't need to turn on the light. I highly recommend black-out curtains. These do not have to be black in color as technology has changed. The colors range from optic white to midnight black. If you windows are not double-pane or energy efficient, these curtains will in effect assist you in keeping the heat in when needed, and the cold air when needed as well. An additional thing you can do is UV protect your windows with window film. These cost about $20.00 at Home Depot and you can install them yourself. It will reflect the light and keep your home climate controlled.

Turn your water heater to 120 degrees. Most people keep these cranked all the way up which is a huge energy waster. Some are even set up so you can add a timer to it. This usually only works if you are single and don't have children. If you are able to do so, and have an electric water heater purchase a $6.00 digital timer and set up the water heater so it only turns on for an hour before you shower each day. Tons of savings. I have not tried this one personally since my water heaters have always been gas, but I understand that it works wonders.

Use only cold water when washing clothing. Hot water does not wash clothes cleaner than cold water. Unless your clothes are infested with lice, bedbugs or mites, you probably don't need hot water. So save the planet, save the money and just wash them in cold.

Give up the dryer or only use it when it is NEEDED. Most of us just toss clothes into the dryer without thinking about it. If you live in a hot climate like me, drying them on the line might take even less time than using the dryer. If not, you can hang a shower curtain rod in the garage or laundry room and hang your clothes on hangers to dry. Another option is a line going from hooks in the back yard. This will save you between $0.50 and $1.00 per load in electricity.

Did you know that the standard electric oven uses between 2,200 and 5,000 watts? A toaster oven uses 1,200 to 1,400 watts. If you are not baking a turkey you can likely make cookies or muffins in a toaster oven and use 1/3 to ½ the electricity in doing so.

Same goes with electric stove tops. They use about 2,200 watts or above. If you can cook outside using foraged wood, go for it. Not only is it delicious but the smoke will add flavor to your meal. While to some it is inconvenient to do so, it is one of my favorite things to do. Almost a hobby.

HEATING AND COOLING

These are probably the biggest electricity users in the household. Most people keep their thermostat at 70 or 72 degrees Fahrenheit for a climate controlled environment. I always wonder how people "survived" without these modern appliances.

Some people say to keep your programmable thermostat a couple degrees warmer in the summer and a couple degrees cooler in the winter to save on electricity. Why not just turn it off, along with the central heater/air conditioner? Try it for a day if the temperatures aren't freezing or frying, but moderate and bearable.

For heat, trying dusting out your fireplace and adding some wood. Not the most efficient, I am aware. If you have a wood stove, this is even better. If so, cruise Craigslist and Facebook Marketplace for free firewood you can use. I was fortunate 2 years ago to fill up a long truck bed full of logs someone wanted to get rid of rather quickly. Lasted me 2 years of constant burning in the winter. About 10 years ago I had a neighbor cut down some giant trees and he was nice enough to give me the firewood. Pine. It burned so hot and smelled so good. I used to dry my clothes around the fireplace just so they could smell like fire until the next washing. I loved it and so did my coworkers. I had 2 girls that would go out of their way to sit next to me on each side of my cubicle. They said the loved the smell so they would always sit by me. It was endearing to them and made them feel like they were at home. Funny how fire can do that to someone.

In really hot climates, evaporative coolers use little electricity and I am told they work wonderfully. Have I tried them? No. I have a high efficiency mini split unit. However, there are evaporative coolers (also known as swamp coolers) that are used for windows and use only 100 watts. These typically cool a room by 20 degrees or so. Why not give it a try? Most central ac units will drain your bank account. However, 100 watts is like two old style light bulbs. That is hardly anything. Many people use these in their off grid properties in desert areas because they use so little in electricity.

When shopping for new appliances, try and get the most energy efficient model you can afford in the style you like. Dishwashers and refrigerators come to mind. When doing a cycle of dishes, make sure to wait until it is completely full and that you use the air-dry function. This will save a minimum of 15% of the energy costs used for a load of dishes. If possible, look for floor model items and look very closely for imperfections in the unit (tiny scratches, tiny dents on the back, etc.). I was able to get $50.00 off my refrigerator this way by seeing a nearly microscopic scratch on the front which was easily covered with a tiny bit of white nail polish. You can no longer see it is there.

When it comes to the refrigerator, it is insane how complicated and large these are becoming. It is like a family is packing to go over the Oregon Trail with how big they make these things now. The average refrigerator size in the United States is 22.5 to 31 cu. ft. In Europe, the average size refrigerator is 10 cu. ft. To anyone reading this from the United States that has not been to Europe, theirs would look like an apartment refrigerator to us. Personally, I have an 11 cu. ft.

refrigerator and am very happy with it. I sometimes think I will build a custom cabinet to put under it to make it taller, and easier to reach the vegetable crisper at the very bottom. I still might. Please just take into consideration the amount of energy you are wasting by storing all that food. You can't fool me. The average household throws away 30% of their food and doesn't even eat it. You don't need a refrigerator that takes up half of your kitchen. If people in Europe can live so small, why can't we? And don't give me "I have kids, you don't understand". They have kids in Europe too.

CHAPTER 15

INHERITANCES AND WINDFALLS

Did you know that the average inheritance is spent within 5 years? That is correct. It is not invested to grow bigger and bigger. It is spent. In many instances, the inheritance is spent on debt or luxury purchases.

I am always jealous around tax time because all of my friends and family end up making thousands of dollars in refunds. For myself (with the exception of 1 year in my adult life), I always owe thousands upon thousands of dollars. Why? Maybe because I am single. Maybe because I have no dependents. Maybe because I have no mortgage to "write-off". However, I would much rather be in the position I am in now (debt free) than using these refunds to pay off debt on money that I have already spent. The average tax refund is $2,727.00. Imagine what you could do if you could just put that in your pocket or do whatever you want with it. You could invest that in an interest bearing account and watch it grow year after year. You could invest in the stock market and possibly double the money within a year. Heck, you could take your family to Disneyland. But no, most people spend their refunds to pay back money that they already spent instead of tightening their belts in the first place so nothing would be owed.

When it comes to an inheritance, it is sad that the average inheritance of a home or assets runs around $68,000.00. Families fight over these dollars and think it will change their life for the better. Statistics say that it won't. It will not change your life. Based on statistics, you will spend it within 5 years. On what? A new boat? A new truck? Spoiling the kids? Good job...you just wasted enough to buy a small house for one of your children.

If you ever receive an inheritance, pretend it is not even there. Call a financial advisor and come up with a plan. Keep the money liquid in case you need it, but do whatever you have to do to make it grow. It should not be sitting there doing nothing, and it should not be spent on junk. This is an amount that can change your family tree and make things better or easier for them. Or you could invest and grow it and give it to charity when you die. Think of how many starving children you could feed. Think of all those cats and dogs that you can keep from being put down. Think of all those homeless people you could feed. There are so many things to do with an inheritance other than just spend it. Be a better person and think of others instead of a stupid new truck.

CLOSING

Here I sit in my new house (paid off) and with over $300k in the bank and another $100k in my retirement savings, which continues to grow each and every month. The $300k in the bank is currently earning a whopping 1% interest, which is $300 a month and pays for my medical insurance and food (which is $216 for medical and $65 for food...yes, I only spend $65 a month on food). Due to the way the economy is right now, the $300k is not invested as I am deciding if I want to wait for a housing correction and move back to California or stay here and live a life free from the rat race and every day stresses. I have nothing but time to decide and make the right financial decision for myself after weighing all the pro's and cons. Please note that my house was purchased as a fixer upper and I have doubled it's value in the 6 months I have lived here. It is important to follow the same example that I provide. I likely will never purchase a move-in ready house because if you do all the work yourself, you can save thousands upon thousands of dollars, even if you hire contractors to do the work.

In closing, this book is intended to be a short and easy read that you can use as a reference in your personal library. Once you start the journey of living on very little, it becomes a game of how little you can live on. Then as your bank account grows and grows each and every month, another game ensues as to how much you can save each month. I wonder if I can save more this month than last month? I wonder if I can find a better interest earning account? I wonder if I can find a credit card that offers better "free" rewards (since you are going to pay it off every month and NEVER keep a balance). I wonder if I can donate and give more this month than last month and still stay within budget. Living the cheap life is a game. A very fun game that most of the population doesn't even know how to play. Others are too busy trying to rob Peter to pay Paul and trying to figure out how they can afford a new car with the little amount of money they are paid. Hopefully you are in a position to never have to worry about that again. If you follow the ideas implemented in this book you are well on your way to becoming a future millionaire. I wish you all the best.